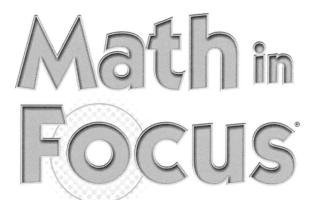

Singapore Math
by Marshall Cavendish

Student Book
Kindergarten (A)
Part 2

Author
Dr. Pamela Sharpe

U.S. Consultants
Andy Clark and Patsy F. Kanter

© 2009 Marshall Cavendish International (Singapore) Private Limited

Published by Marshall Cavendish Education
An imprint of Marshall Cavendish International (Singapore) Private Limited
Times Centre, 1 New Industrial Road, Singapore 536196
Customer Service Hotline: (65) 6411 0820
E-mail: tmesales@sg.marshallcavendish.com
Website: www.marshallcavendish.com/education

Distributed by
Houghton Mifflin Harcourt
222 Berkeley Street
Boston, MA 02116
Tel: 617-351-5000
Website: www.hmheducation.com/mathinfocus

First published 2009

Marshall Cavendish and *Math in Focus®* are trademarks of Times Publishing Limited.

Math in Focus® Kindergarten A Part 2
ISBN 978-0-669-01113-5

Printed in China

7 8   1401   16 15 14 13 12
4500373238   B C D E

Contents

Lesson 1 'Small', 'Medium', and 'Big'

Look and talk.

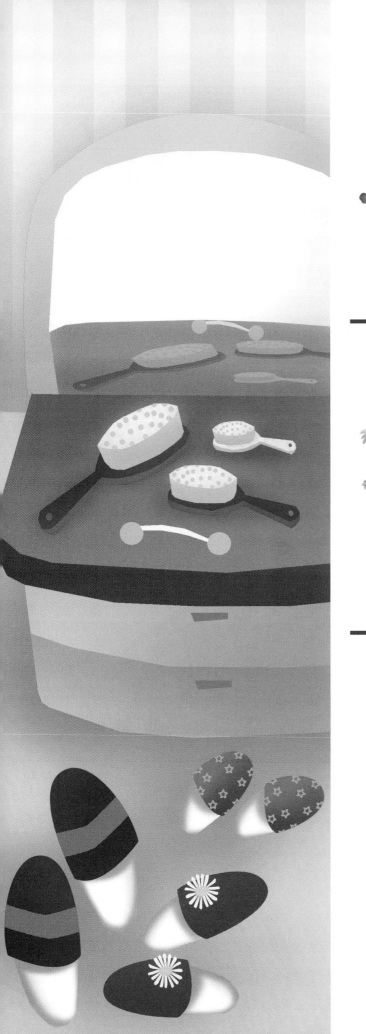

Which brush is Baby Bear's?

The yellow one is Baby Bear's.

Whose red bathrobe is it?

It is Mama Bear's.

Which pillow is the biggest?

The blue one is the biggest.

Trace.

The mother duck is first.

The brown duckling is next to the white duckling.

The black duckling is in between the two white ducklings.

Color to complete the pattern.

Trace.

Trace. Look for a pattern.

Which is the heaviest? Circle.

Color to complete the pattern.

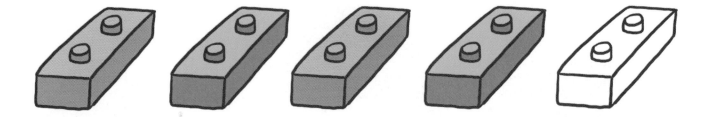

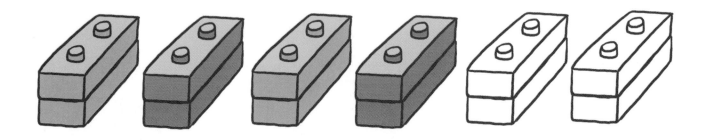

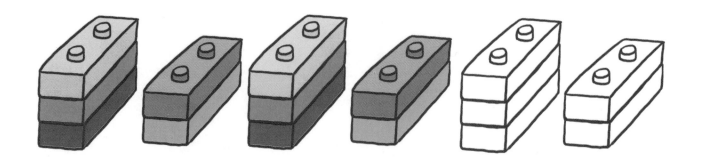

4 Counting and Numbers 0 to 10

Lesson 1 Counting Things One-to-One Up to 10

Sing.

4 red apples
big and juicy,

Sitting in a bowl
for all to see,

Waiting for my friends
and me,

4 red apples
big and juicy.

Count and write.

Draw one more. Count and write.

Draw, count, and write.

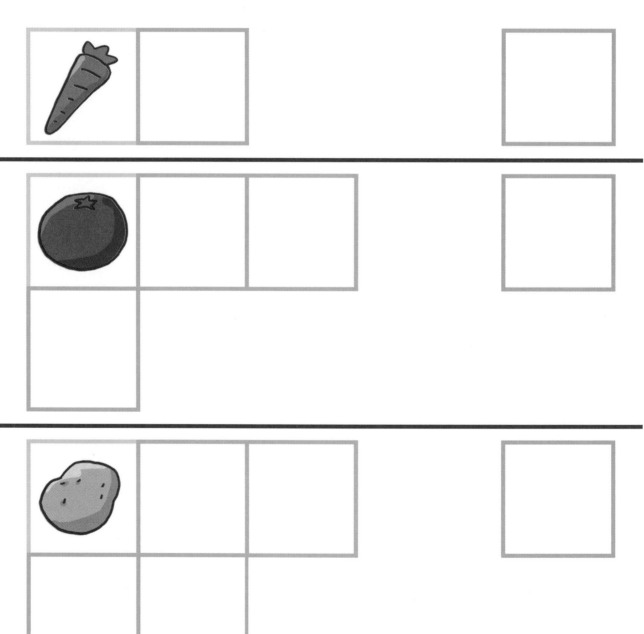

Count and write.

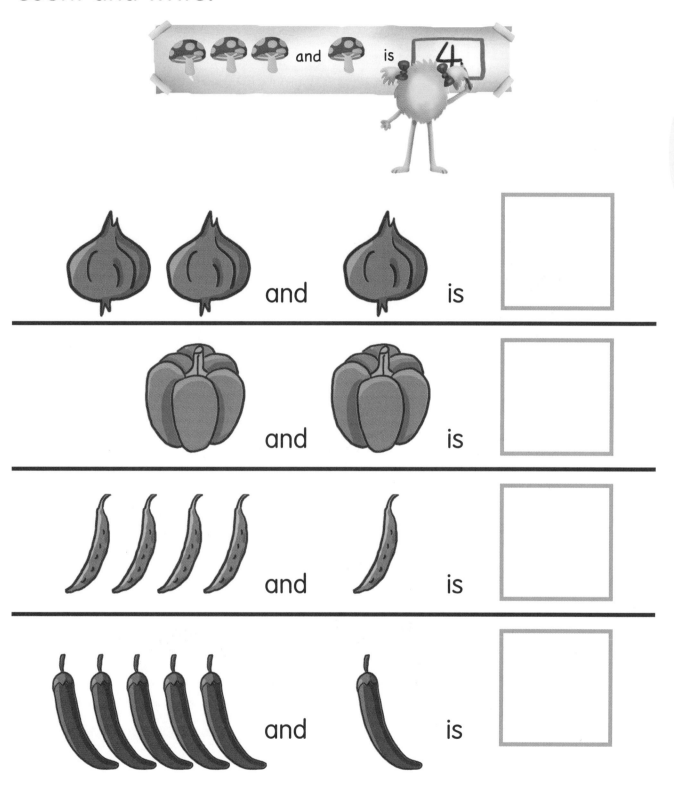

Sing.

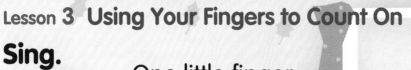

One little finger,
one little finger,

One little finger,
tap, tap, tap.

Point to the ceiling,

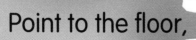

Point to the floor,

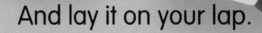

And lay it on your lap.

Count and write.

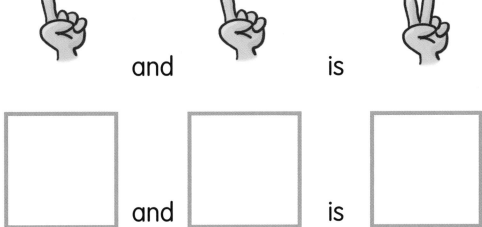

Count and write.

 and is

[ ] and [ ] is [ ]

 and is

[ ] and [ ] is [ ]

 and is

[ ] and [ ] is [ ]

Let's play!

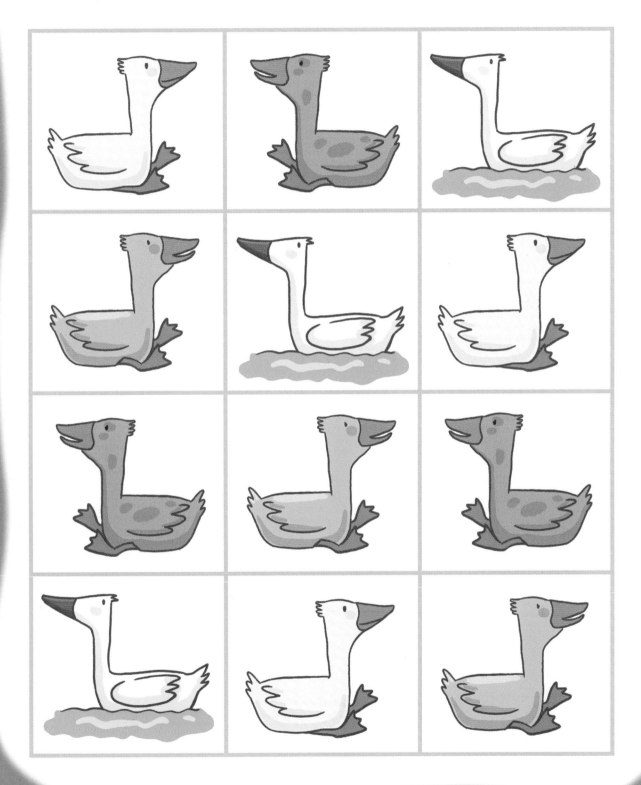

19

Look and talk.

How many more? Count and write.

Lesson 7 Less Than
Count and write.

_____ more flowers are needed.

_____ more flowers are needed.

_____ more flowers are needed.

Circle.

Which group has fewer than 3?

Which group has fewer than 5?

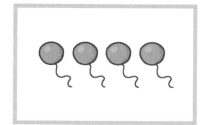  

Which group has fewer than 7?

  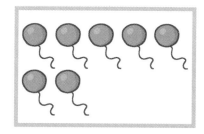

Which group has fewer than 9?

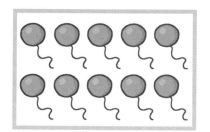  

Lesson 8 How Many in All?

Draw.

Draw 0 ● .

Draw 1 ○ .

Draw 2 ○ s.

Draw 3 ● s.

Draw 4 ● s.

Draw 5 ⚪ s.

Draw 6 🔘 s.

Draw 7 🔘 s.

Draw 8 ⚫ s.

Draw 9 ⚪ s.

Draw 10 🔘 s.

Draw one more. How many are there in all?

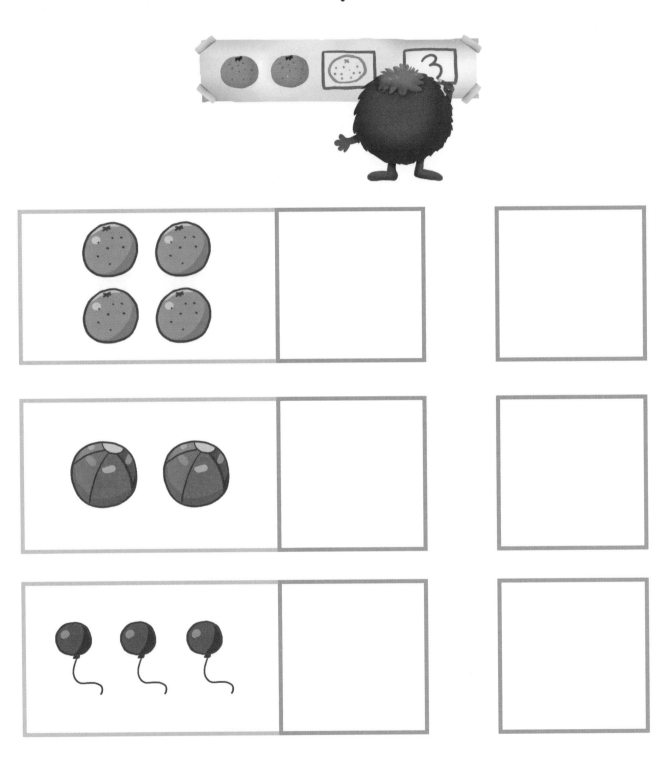

Circle, count, and write.

Circle sets of 3.

---

2 birds fly away. Circle the birds that stay behind.

_____ birds stay behind.

---

4 horses trot away. Circle the horses that stay behind.

_____ horses stay behind.

Chapter 5

Size and Position

Lesson 1 Big and Small Things

Draw.

Lesson 3 Does It Fit?
Count and write.

Count and write.

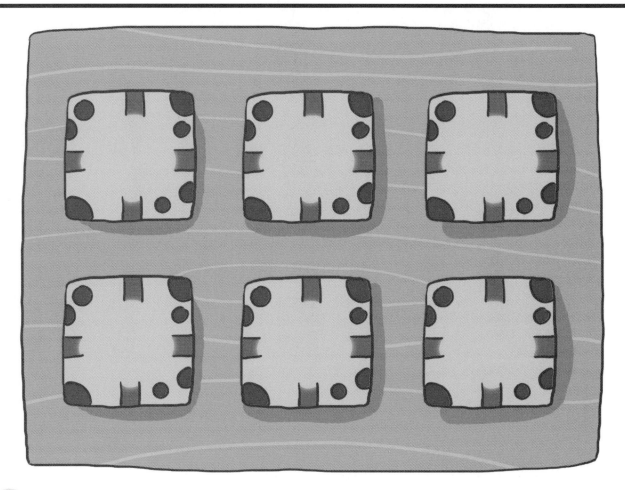

Pair.

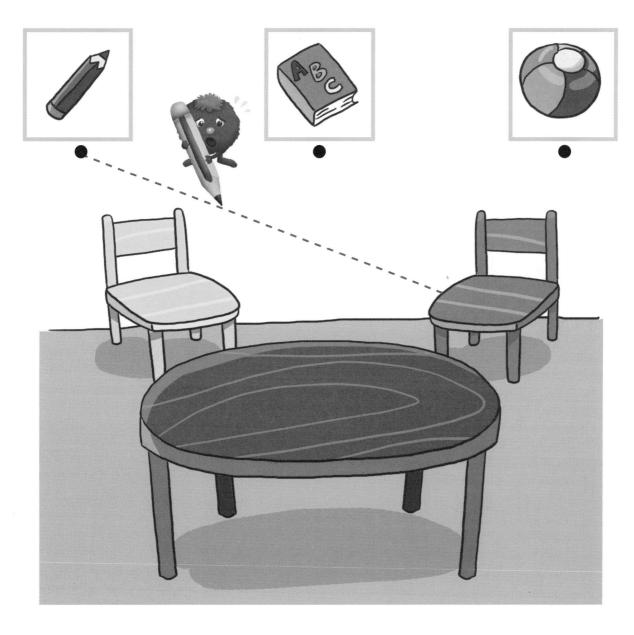

Lesson 5 'Before' and 'After'

Color the box.

Before	After

Before	After

Before	After

Before	After

What do you do before breakfast? Color.

What do you do after school? Color.

Counting and Numbers to 20

Lesson 1 Numbers to 20
Count and write.

Sing.

One, two, buckle my shoe

Three, four, knock the door

Five, six, pick up sticks

Seven, eight, lay them straight

Nine, ten, a big fat hen

Eleven, twelve,
Dig and delve

Thirteen, fourteen,
Maids a-sorting

Fifteen, sixteen,
Maids in the kitchen

Seventeen, eighteen,
Maids a-waiting

Nineteen, twenty,
My plate's empty!

Count and write.

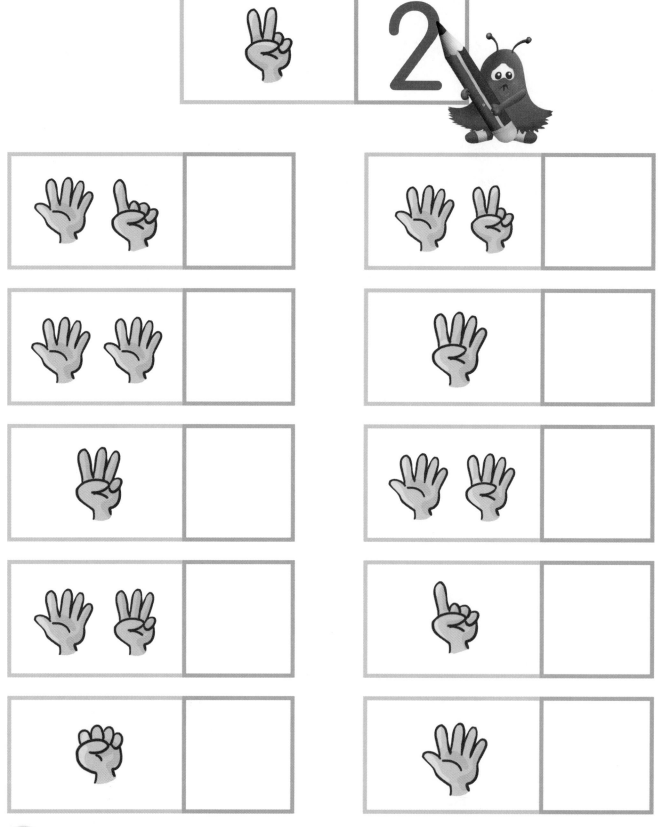

Fill in the missing numbers.

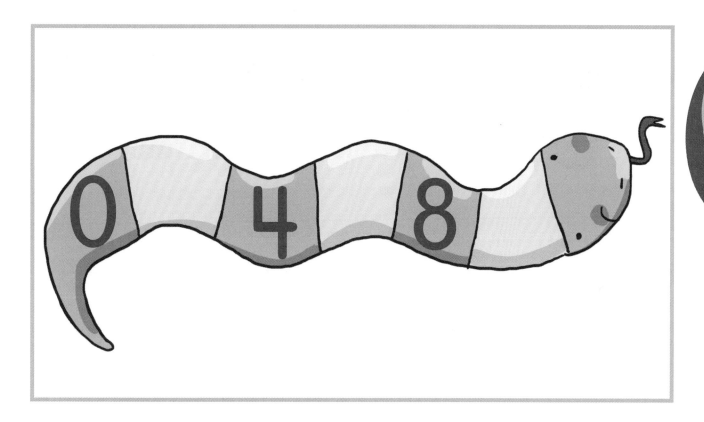

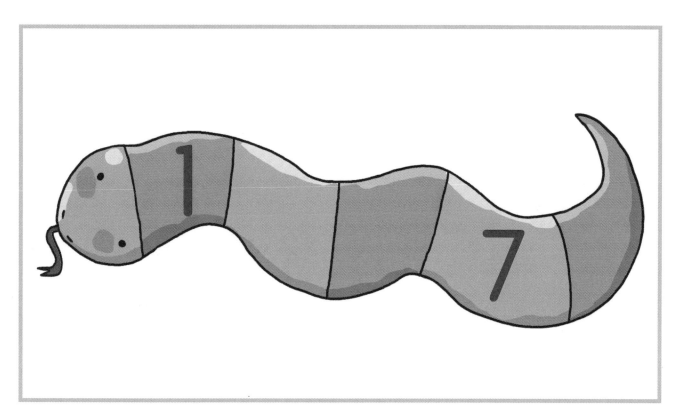

Lesson 6 Finding More
Count and write.

How many more apples do we need? _____

 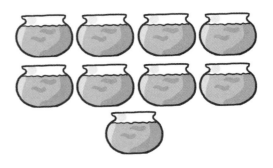

How many more fish do we need? _____

How many more balloons do we need? _____

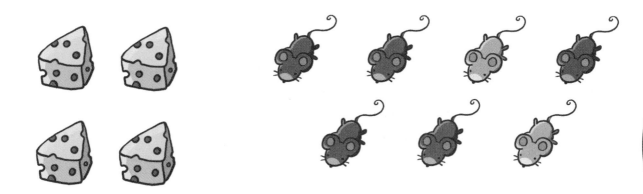

How many more pieces of cheese do we need? _____

How many more worms do we need? _____

How many more carrots do we need? _____

Lesson 7 Number Stories Using 'One More'

Read, count, and write.

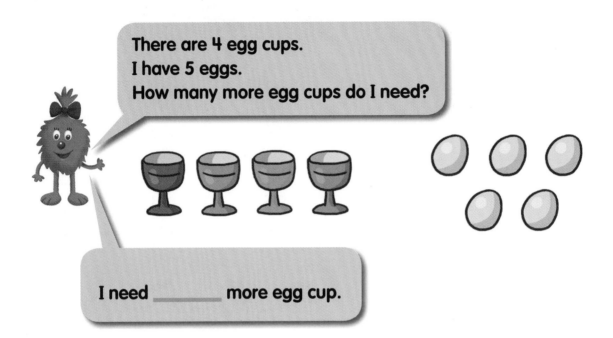

There are 4 egg cups.
I have 5 eggs.
How many more egg cups do I need?

I need _____ more egg cup.

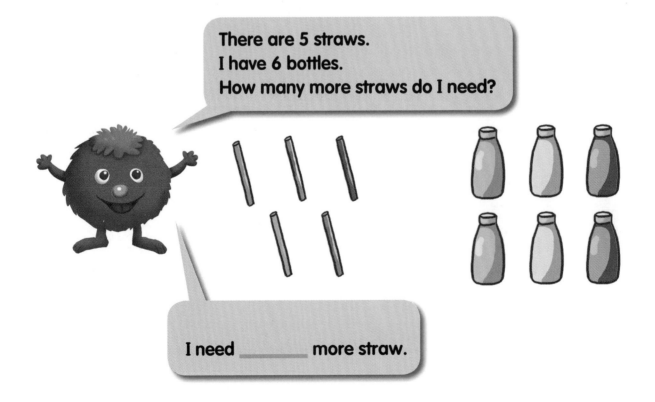

There are 5 straws.
I have 6 bottles.
How many more straws do I need?

I need _____ more straw.

There are 2 bowls.
I have 3 spoons.
How many more bowls do I need?

I need _____ more bowl.

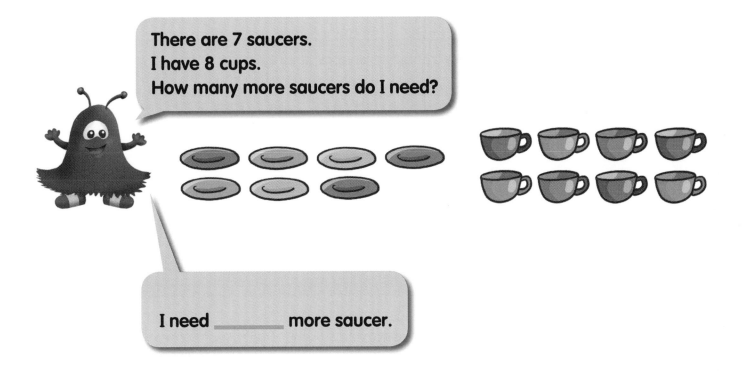

There are 7 saucers.
I have 8 cups.
How many more saucers do I need?

I need _____ more saucer.